MARJORY'S BOOK

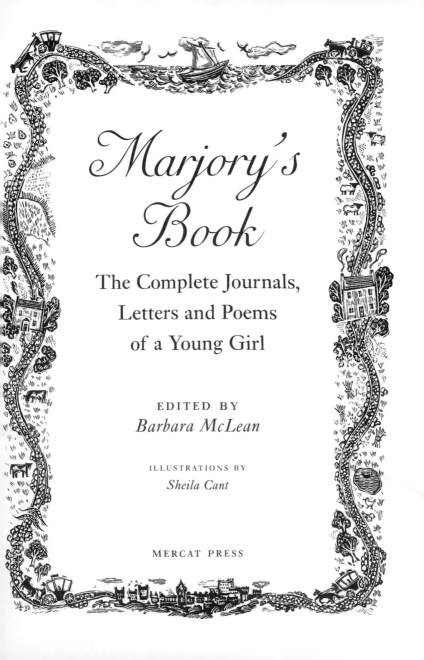

Marjory's Book

The Complete Journals, Letters and Poems of a Young Girl

EDITED BY
Barbara McLean

ILLUSTRATIONS BY
Sheila Cant

MERCAT PRESS

First published
in 1999 by Mercat Press
James Thin,
53 South Bridge,
Edinburgh EH1 1YS

ISBN 1 873644 96 5

Set in Ehrhardt
Book design by Mark Blackadder

Printed and bound in Great Britain by
The Cromwell Press.

§ CONTENTS §

Dedicated to M.rs H. Crawfurd by the

Three Turkeys fair their last have t...

And now this worted for ever travea...

Their Father & their Mother too

Will sigh & weep as well as you

Mourning for their osprings fair

Whom they did nurse with tender c...

Indeed the rats their bones have crav...

To eternity are they launched

Their graceful form & pretty ey...

Their fellow pows did not despise

A direful death indeed they had

That would put any parent in...

But she was more then usual cal...

She did not give a single dam...

She was gentle as a lamb

Here ends this melancholy la...

§ ACKNOWLEDGEMENTS §

I am indebted to Alan Rankin, dealer in rare books and manuscripts, for first introducing me to Marjory Fleming. Thanks also to Gavin Grant, Assistant Curator of Kirkcaldy Art Gallery and Museum and to the staff of the North Reading Room, National Library of Scotland.

All examples from Marjory's Journals are reproduced courtesy of the National Library of Scotland.

§ NOTES ON TEXT §

The three journals, each measuring 7½" by 8", were ruled throughout by Isabella Keith as an aid to Marjory's handwriting. Isabella corrected her pupil's spelling mistakes and omissions, but in the interests of clarity these additions and Isabella's rare marginal comments (such as 'fie!') have been excluded. Square brackets – for example: love your neighbour & he will [love] you – indicate missing letters, and in the original these mostly occur at the end of a line where Marjory ran out of space. Pages that have been cut, most common in the second journal, are identified in the Notes.

§ FOREWORD §

Marjory Fleming lived her short life in Scotland in the early years of the nineteenth century. She was born in Kirkcaldy in 1803 and died there after a bout of measles just before she reached the age of nine.

For a time she lived with relations in Edinburgh, and was there educated by her older cousin Isabella, who required her young charge to keep a regular journal so that the developing skills of handwriting, spelling and punctuation could be observed and corrected. Between 1810 and 1811, when Marjory was seven and eight, she filled three slim notebooks with her own individual observations and poems, encompassing topics as diverse as literature, love, history and religion. They were intended for an audience no wider than her tutor and her immediate family. But after her death, all her papers were carefully preserved, and eventually they found their way into print. (The story of that piecemeal progress is told in the Afterword.) As a result, she achieved a posthumous reputation that earned her a place in the *Dictionary of National Biography* (the youngest author ever to be recorded) and tributes from Robert Louis Stevenson and Mark Twain.

To read Marjory's journals is to glimpse a vanished world and, much more than that, it is to bring to life an extraordinary child and reawaken all the 'thunderstorms and sunshine' of her engaging personality.

FIRST JOURNAL
Spring and Summer,
1810

Many people are hanged for Highway robbery Housebreking Murder &c &c

Isabella teaches me everything I know and I am much indebted to her she is learnen witty & sensible. I can but make a poor reward for the servises she has done me if I can give her any but I doubt it.

Repent & be wise saith the preacher before it be to late.

Regency bnnets are become very fashionable of late & every[body] gets them save poor me but if I had one it would not become me.

A Mirtal is a beautifull plant & so is a Geramem & nettel Geramem[1]

Climbing is a talent which the bear excels in and so does monkeys apes & baboons.

I have been washing my dools cloths today & I like it very much

People who have a good Concience is alwa[ys] happy but those who have a bad one is always unhappy & discontented

There is a dog that yels continualy & I pity him to the bottom of my heart indeed I do.

Tales of fashionable life[2] ar very good storys Isabella campels me to sit down & not to rise till this page is done but it is very near finished only one line to write

*

Yesterday the thunder roared & now and then flashes of lightning was seen but today their is no such thing & far from it, for it is very warm sunny & mild.

The Monkey gets as many visitors as I or my cousins.

Nobody can be happy that has guilt on his mind. Grandeur & Magnificence makes one Proud & Insolent peevish & petish & these make us miserable & unhappy besides people will hate us & abhor us and dispise us We should get the better of our passion & not let then get the bet[ter of us]

Osians poems[3] are most beautiful. —I am very strong & robust & not of the delicate sex nor of the fair but of the deficent in look People who are deficient in looks can make up for it by virtue.

I am very fond of the Arabin nights entertainments & wish to read the tales of the Genie. Silver & Gould is ve[ry] presous. —I am fair as the sun & beautiful as the moon.

I hear many people speak about the Exebition[4] and I long very much to behold it but I have to little money to pay the expence. – Queen streat is a very gay one & so is Princes streat for all the lads & lases besides bucks & beggars parade there.

Tomsons him to the seasons[5] is most eligant & most beautifull & so is young Celidon & his Emelia but is melancholy & distresing poor man his fate was a dismale he was an unhappy lover

A Mr Burn writs a beautifull song on a Mr Cunhaming[6] whose wife desarted hin truly it is a most beautifull one

I like to read the Fabulous historys[7] about the historys of Robin Dickey flapsay & Peccay & it is very amuseing for some were good birds and others bad but Peccay was the most dutifull & obedient to her parents

I went into Isabellas bed to make her smile like the Genius Demedicus[8] the statute in ancient Grece but she fell asleep in my very fa[ce] at which my anger broke forth so that I awoke her from a very comfortable nap all was now hushed up but agan my anger burst forth a[t] her biding me get up

I have read in the history of Scotland how Murry the regent was shot by Hamilton of Bothwellhaugh but Murry used Hamiltons wife very ill & drove her quite mad but Hamilton should have left Murrys punishment to God Almighty for revenge is a very bad thing & aught not to be done

Many people are so sinful as to steal & murder but they have punishment either from God or men in this world or the next In the New whole duty of men, that says that familly prayer should be well atended to.

I should like to see a play very much for I never saw one in all my life & dont believe I ever shall but I hope I can be content without going to one I con be quite happy without my desire be granted People should set others an exampal of doing good for every body is happy that doeth good

Nancys and Isabellas uncle has got Musical Glases & the sound of them is exceeding sweet. —The poetical works of tomas Grey are most beautifull espacially one the death of a favourite Cat who was drowned in a Tub of fishes. —When books are funy & amuseing I am very fond of them such as the araiban nights entertaintents & the Tales of the Castal[9] &c &c. Every body should be unasuming & not asuming. —We should regard virtue but not vice for that leads us to distriction & makes us unhappy all our life

Some days ago Isabella had a tereable fit of the toothake and she walked with a long nightshift at dead of night like a gost and [I] thought she was one she prayed for, tired natures sweet restorer bamy sleep but did not get it a ghostly figure she was indeed enought to ma[ke] a saint tremble it made me quever & shake from top to toe but I soon got the beeter of it & next morning I quite forgot it

Superstition is a very very mean thing & should be dispised & shuned

AN ADRESS TO
MY FATHER WHEN HE CAME
TO EDINBURGH

My father from Kercaldy ca[me]
But not to plunder or to game
Gameing he shuns I am very surre
For he has a hart that is very pure
Honest & well behaved is he
And busy as a little Bee

I am very fond of some parts of Tomsons seasons. —I like loud Mirement & laughter. —I love to walk in lonely solitude & leave the bustel of the nosey town behind me & while I look on nothing but what strikes the eye with sights of bliss & then I think myself transported far beyond the reach of the wicked sons of men where there is nothing but strife & envying pilefring & murder where neither contentment nor retirement dweels but their dwels drunken[ness]

Beautious Isabella say
How long at breahead will you stay
O for a week or not so long
Then weel desart the busy throng
Ah can you see me sorrow so
And drop a hint that you must go
I thought you had a better hart
Then make me with my dear friends [part]
But now I see that you have not
And that you mock my dreadful lot
My health is always bad and sore[10]
And you have hurt it a deal more

The reason I write this poem is because I am going to Breahead only two days

*

I like to here my own sex praised but not the other. —The vision is most beautiful Breahead is a beautiful place & on a charming situation

I should like to see the Exibition very much & still more so the theater

I am reading the misteris of udolpho[11] with Isabella & am much interested with them I have got some of Popes works by hart & like them very much.

The days are very long and very light just now which is very pleasant to me & I darsay to every body

I should like to go and see the curosities in Londen but I should be a little affr[aid] of the robbers For that country is greatly infested with them at Edinburgh their is not so many of them

There is a very nice book called The Monk & the Vinedresser written by a lady but I do not know her name

It is true that

Death the rightious love to see

But from it doth the wicked flee

I am sure they fly as fast as their legs can carry them

My cousin John has a beautiful musaim & he has got many nice curiosities

*

Macbeth is a fearful play.

I pityed Mary Queen of Scots when the people held a standard on which was painted the dead King and his son kneeling and uttering these words judge & revenge my cause O Lord. I should not liked to have been her but I think it was very wrong in the people to mock their sovereign & queen I have seen her picture & think her most Beautiful & Angelick Elisbeth behaved very crually to poor poor Mary

*

Today O today I am going to Breahead but alas my pleasure will be soon damped for I must com home in too days but I wish to stay too months or more for I am very fond of the country and could stay at Breahead all my life There the wind houles to the waves dashing roar but I would not we[ep] my woes there upon any account

THE KINGS BIRTHDAY[12]

To days ago was the Kings Birthday
And to his health we sung a lay
Poor man his health is very bad
And he is often very mad
He was a very comely lad
Since death took his girl from his si[ght]
He to her grave doth walk at night
His son the grand grard Duke [of York]
I'm sure he eateth plenty pork
For I do hear that he is fat
But I am not so sure of that

Of summer I am very fond
And love to baith into a pond
The look of sunshine dies away
And will not let me out to play
I love the morning sun to see
That makes me from the house to flee
I love the morning sun to spy
Glittring through the casements eye
The rays of light are very sweet
And puts away our taste of meat

My lover Isa walks with me
And then we sing a prity glee
My lover I am sure shes not
But we are content with our lot
Often I have heard people say
In the right path I love to stray
But wickedness I cannot bear
To walk with it I will not dare

The trees do wave their lofty heads while the winds stupendous breath wafts the scattered leaves afar off besides the declifities of the rocks leaves that once was green and beautifull now withered and all wed away scatering their remains on the footpath and highroads &c &c

The balmy brease comes down from heaven
And makes us like for to be living
But when we [think] that if we died
No pleasure there would be denied
There happiness doth always reign
And there we feel not a bit pain
In the morning the first thing I see
Is most beautiful trees spreading their luxurant branches
between the Horison & me

There is a thing I love to see
That is our monkey catch a flee
With loks that shews that he is prou[d]
He gathers round him such a crowd
But if we scold he will grin
And up he..ll jump and make a din

I love to see the morning sun that rises so long before the
moon the moon that casts her silver light whe[n] the
Horison sinks beneath the cloud and scateres its light on
the surface of the earth;

Here at Breahead I enjoy rurel filisity to perfection,
content, retirement rurel quiet frienship books, all these
dweel here but I am not sure of ease and alternate labour
useful life

ISAS BED

I love in Isas bed to lie
O such a joy & luxury
The botton of the bed I sleep
And with great care I myself keep
Oft I embrace her feet of lillys
But she has goton all the pillies
Her neck I never can embrace
But I do hug her feet in place
But I am sure I am contented
And of my follies am repented
I am sure I'd rather be
In a smal bed at liberty

*

At Breahead I lay at the foot of the bed[13] becase Isabella says that I disturbed her repose at night by contunial fighting and kicking but I was very well contunaly at work reading the Arabin nights entertainments which I could not have done had I slept at the top. I am reading the Mysteries of udolpho & am much interested in the fate of poor poor Emily

ON JESSY WATSONS ELOPEMENT

Run of is Jessy Watson fair
Her eyes do sparkel she's good hair
But Mrs Leath you shal now be
Now and for all Etenity
Such merry spirits I do hate
But now its over and to late
For to retract such vows you cant
And you must now love your galant
But I am sure you will repent
And your poor hart will then rela[nt]
Your poor poor father will repine
And so would I if you werc mine
But now be good for this time past
And let this folly be your last

FAIR PHILLIP

Oar hills & dales fair Phillip strayes
And he doth walk through all the ways
He and myselfe are lovers true
We can feal pangs as well as you
Those that feal pangs are not so few
We walked upon the distand hills
And often goes into the mills
Very soft and wite his cheeks

His hair is fair & grey his breaks
His teath is like the daisy fair
The only fault is on his hair
I am beginning to be jealous
And feel a small degree of malice
That kindeles in my bosom fair
And fills my hart with great despair
Ah man you said you once loved m[e]
But from your promises you flee

*

The sun is seen glimering through the trees whose spreading foilage allows only a slight tinge to be seen it is a Beautiful sight

In the dining room & drawing at Breahea[d] The walls are hung with the pictures of there ancestors both men and weomen

The hedges are green the trees are green & every thing bears a pleasure to the eye when we look on them

Thre is some beautiful trees behind the house & before the house which makes it very

*

I have been a Naughty Girl
I have been a Naughty Girl[14]

*

The lofty trees their heads do shake
When the wind blows, a noise they make
When they are cut a crash you hear
That fills your very soul with fear
Tis like the thunders loudest roar
You would not like to hear much more
It makes the earth begin to quake
And all its mity pillers shake
The viabration of the sound
Will I am sure you quit[e] confound
It makes the mountains to resound

THREE TURKEYS
Dedicated to Mrs H Crawfurd
by the author MF

Three Turkeys fair their last have breathed
And now this worled for ever leaved
Their Father & their Mother too
Will sigh & weep as well as you
Mourning for thre osprings fair
Whom they did nurse with tender care
Indeed the rats their bones have cranched
To eternity are they launched
There graceful form & pretty eyes
Their fellow pows did not despise[15]
A direful death indeed they had

That would put any parent mad
But she was more then usual calm
She did not give a singel dam
She is as gentel as a lamb
Here ends this melancholy lay
Farewell poor Turkeys I must say

Tis, eve, the wind is very boisterous the sea must be very
tempestious while the waves montain high dashes in the
ships side overturnes it & launches the crew into eternity

I LOVE TO SEE

I love to see the mornings light
That glitters through the trees so bright
Its splended rays indeeds full sweet
And takes away our tast of meat
I love to see the moon shine bright
It is a very nobel sight
Its worth to sit up all the night
But I am going to my tea
And what I'v said is not a lee

*

[P]oor Williams gone to Giffords fair
To see the things that are seen there
I'm sure he will be much amused
For to such things he is not used
There lads and & lasses he will see
Dressed as gay as can sure be

I have been often at a fair & am alwys very much interested & amused with it ther are always a great concorse of people at it

Here I pas my life in rurel filicity festivity & pleasure I saunter about the woods & forests

Breahead is far far sweeter then Edinburgh or any other place Everything is beautiful some colour is red others green & white &c &c but the Trees & hedges are the most beautiful for they are of the most pretty green I ever beheld in all my life

*

Goodness of hart gentelness & meekness make one beloved & respected by those who are acquainted with them but pride insolence and bad hartedness is always hated and despised it is better to follow after the first then after the last for the first is good and the last is bad

*

Of sauntering about the doors I am very fond especialy when it is a fine & sunny day. I am very fond of Spring Summer & Autun but I am not so fond of winter for then it is cold & dreeiry

*

Isabella says that when we pray we should pray fervently & not rattel over a praye[r] when our thoughts are wandering but to collect our thoughts for that we are kneeling at the footstool of our Lord &⸱creator who we ought to respect honour & obey with due revirance & fear he created us & he may take away our blisings if he pleaes

He showers down blissings on our heads when we least deserve them & forgives our sins & forgetfulness of him our Lord & creator who saved us from mesiry & eternal damnation, from unquestionable fire & brimston he saved us

BED

When cold as clay when cold as ice
To get into a bed tis nice
It is a nice thing for to creep
But not to dose away & sleep
Into a bed where Isa lies
And to my questions she replies
Corrects my faults improves my mi[nd]
And teels me of the faults she find
But she is soun asleep sometimes
For that I have not got good rhy[mes]
But when awake I her teize mu[ch]
And she doth squall at every touch
Then Isa reads in bed alone
And reads the fasts by good Nelson[16]
Then I get up to say my prayers
To get my porridge & go down stairs

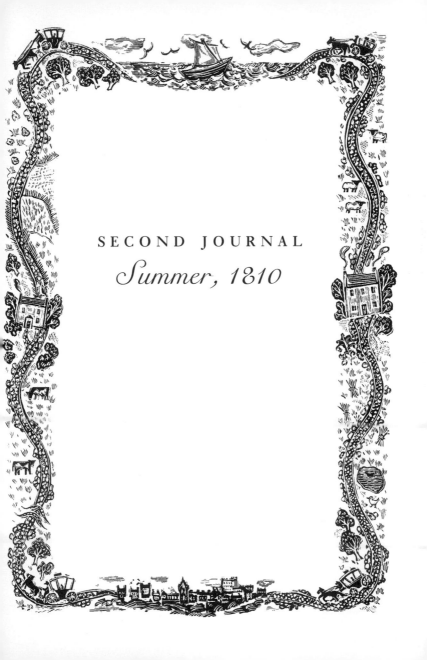

SECOND JOURNAL
Summer, 1810

The Day of my existence here has been delightful & enchantinting.[1] On Saturday I expected no less than three well made Bucks the names of whom is here advertised Mr. Geo Crakey and Wm Keith and Jn Keith, the first is the funniest of every one of them Mr. Crakey & I walked to Crakeyhall[2] han by hand in Innocence and matitation sweet thinking on the kind love which flows in out tenderhearted mind which is overflowsing with majestick pleasu[re] nobody was ever so polite to me in the hole state of my existence. Mr Craky you must know is a great Buck & pretty goodlooking

*

I am at Ravelston enjoying natures fresh air the birds are sining sweetly the calf doth frisk and play and nature shows her glorious face. The sun shines through the trees, it is delightful

*

§   WEDNESDAY. . . THURSDAY 1 2 JULY[3] §

I confess that I have been more like a little young Devil then a creature for when Isabella went up the stairs to teach me religion and my multiplication and to be good and all my other lessons I stamped with my feet and threw my new hat which she made on the ground and was sulky an was dreadfuly passionate but she never whiped

me but gently said Marjory go into another room and think what a great crime you are committing and letting your temper git the better of you but I went so sulkely that the Devil got the better of me but she never never whip me so that I thinke I would be the better of it and the next time that I behave ill I think she should do it for she never does it but she is very indulgent to me but I am very ungratefll to hir

*

To Day I have been very ungrateful and bad and dis-obedient Isabella gave me my writing I wrote so ill that she took it away and locted it up in her desk where I stood trying to open[5] it till she made me come and read my bible but I was in a bad honour and red it so Carelessly and ill that she took it from me and her blood ran cold but she never punished me she is as gental as a lamb. to me an ungrateful girl

*

Isabella has given me praise for checking my temper for I was sulkey when she was kneeling an hole hourr teachin me to write

*

Yesterday I behave extreme ill in Gods most holy church for I would never attand myself nor let Isabella attand which was a great crime for she often often tells me that when to or three are geathered together G[od] is in the midst of them and it was the very same Divel that tempted Job that tempted me I am sure but he resisted satan though he had boils and many many other misfortunes which I have escaped.–

*

I am now going to tell you about the horrible and wret[ched] plaege that my multiplication gives me you cant concieve it – the most Devilish thing is 8 times 8 & 7 times 7 it is what nature itselfe cant endure[6]

∗

I have a delightl pleasure in view which is the thoughts of going to Braehead where I will walk to Craky-hall wich puts me In mind that I walked to that delightfull place with that delightfull young man beloved by all his friends and espacialy by me his loveress but I must not talk any longer about hin any longer for Isa said it is not proper for to speak of gentalm[en] but I will never forget him

∗

I hope that at 12 or 13 years old I will be as learned as Miss Isa and Nancy Keith for many girls have not the advantage I have and I [am] very very glad that satan has not geven me boils and many other Misfortunes, in the hly bible these words are written that the Devel goes abou like a roaring lyon in search of his pray but the lord lets us escape from him but we sometimes do not strive with this aufull spirit

∗

To Day I bronounced a word which should never come out of a ladys lips it was that I caled John a Impudent

Bitch and [Isabella] afterwards told me that I should never say it even in joke but she kindly forgave me because I said that I would not do it again I will tell you wha I think made me in so bad a homour is I got 1 or 2 cups of that bad bad sina tea[7] to Day

*

Last night I behaved extremely ill and threw my work in the stairs and would not pick it up which was very wrong indeed; and all that William could do I would not go out of the room till he himself put me out and [I] roar like a bull and would not go to bed though Isabella bid me go which was very wrong indeed to her when she takes so much pains with me when she would like best to be walking but she thinks it her duty

*

As this is Sunday I must begin to write serious thoughts as Isabella bids me. I am thinking how I should Impro[ve] the many talents I have. I am very sory I have thrown them away it is shoking to think of it when have many have half the instruction I have the because Isabella teaches me to or three hours every day in reading and writing and arethmatick and many other things and religion into the bargan. On Sunday she teaches me to be virtuos

*

Ravelston is a fine pla[ce] because I got balm win and many other dain[ties] and extremely pleasan to me by the companied of swine geese cocks &c and they are the delight of my heart.

I was at a race to Day & like it very much but we mi[ssed] one of the starts which was ve[ry] provoaking indeed but I cannot help it so I must not complain lord Mongumorys horse gained it but I am clattering so I will tur[n] the subject to another think; – but no I must git my spelling first I acknowledge that this page is far from being well written

*

Isabella teaches me my lessons from ten till two every day and I wonder she is not tired to death with me for my part I would be quite Impatient if I had a child to teach.

It was a dreadfull thing that Haman was hanged on a garows which he had prepared for Mordica to hang him & his ten sons thereon & it was very wrong & crua[l] to hang his sons because they did not commit the crime but then Jesus was not then come to teach us to be Mercifull; ,[8]

*

Yesterday I behaved excee[dingly] ill & what is Worse of all is when Isabella told me not to let my temper get the better of me but I did not mind her & sinned away which was very nauty;

*

Yesterday then thunder bolts roled Mightiy oer the hils it was very Majestick, but to Day there has been no thunder, but I will speak about another thing; .

Yesterday I am very glad to say a young Cocker came to our house to stay, it is very beautifu[l] & it is named Crakey it was Isabella that na[med] him & white & black is its coualer but all the wh[ite] will come of is not that wonderfull; ,

*

This is Saturday, & I am very glad of it, because I have play half of the Day, & I get mony too, but alas I owe Isabella 4 pence, for I am finned 2 pence whenever I bite my n[ails]

*

Isa is teaching me to make Simecolings nots of interr-gations peorids & commoes &c;

As this is Sunday I will Meditate uppo[n] Senciable & Religious subjects first I should be very thankful that I am not a begger as many are; .

I get my poetry now out of grey & I thin[k] it beautiful & Majestick but I am sorry to say that I thi[nk] it is very Difficult to get by heart but we mus bear it well;

I hope that Isabella will have the goodness to teach me Geogrifie Mathematicks & Fractions &c.;[9]

The Scythians tribe lives very corsly for a Gluton Introdused to Arsaces the Captai[n] of the Armey, 1 man who Dressed hair & another man who was a good cook but Araces said that he would keep 1 for brushing his horses tail, & the other to fead his pigs;

*

Dear Isa is very indulgent to me, for which usage I am sorrow to say, that I am always do[in]g something or other ill, which is very nauty, is it not,;

It is Malancholy to think, that I hav so many talents, & many there are that have not had the attention paid to them that I have, & yet they contrive to [be] better then me; Mrs Craford has a dog & I believ it is as beautifull as any in good Old England, I am sure; & she had 5 pups but they are all drowned but 1 ;

Now I am quite happy : for I am going tomorrow to a delightfull place, Breahead by name, belonging to Mrs Crraford, where their is ducks cocks hens bublyjocks[10] 2 dogs 2 cats swine. & which is delightful; I thing it is shoking to think that the dog & cat should bear them &

they are drowned after all I would rather have a man dog then a women dog because they do not bear like women dogs, it is a hard case it is shoking; –

I came here as I thought to enjoy natures delightful breath it is sweeter than a fial of rose Oil but Alas my hopes are dissoopinted, it is always spitring but then I often get a blink & than I am happy[11]

*

Every Morn I awake before Isa & Oh I wish to be up & out with the turkies but I must take care of Isa who when aslipe is as beautifull as Viness & Jupiter in the skies;

*

To Day I affronted myself before Miss Margret & Miss Isa Craford Mrs Craford & Miss Kermical which was very nauty but I hope that there will be no more evel in all my Journal;

*

To Day is Saturday & I sauntered about the woulds & by the burn sid & dirtied myselfe which puts me in mind of a song my mother conp[o]sed it was that she was out & dirtied herself which is like me;

I am very sory to say that I forgot God that is to say I forgot to pray today & Isabella told me that I should be thankful tha he did not forget me if he did O what would become of me if I was in danger & God not friends with me I must go to unquenchiable fire & if I was tempted to sin how could I resist it I will never do it again no no not if I can help it;

*

I am going to tell you of a malancholy story A young Turkie of 2 or 3 month Old would you believe it the father broak its leg & he kiled another I think he should be transported or hanged;

Will the sarvent has buried the Turkie & put a tomeston & written this is in memory of the young Turke

*

I am going to tell you that in all my life I never behaved so ill for when Isa bid me go out of the room I would no go & when Isa came to the room I threw my book at her in a dreadful passion & she did not lick me but said go into room & pray & I did it I will never do it again I hope that I will never afront Isa for she said that shs was never so afronted in her life but I hope it will nevr happen again[12]

*

We expect Nancy tomorrow I am happy she is coming but I would be still happer if I behaved better but I will be better;

*

I got a young bird & I have tamed it & it hopes on my finger. Alas I have promised it to Miss Bonner & the cage is here & little Dickey is in it; How O how shal I receive Nancy after behaving so ill. I tremble at it, it is dreadful to think of it, it is; I am going to turn over a new life & am going to be a very good girl & be obedient to Isa Keith,

Here there is planty of goosberys which makes my teath watter;

Yesterday there was campony Mr & Mrs Bonner & Mr Philip Caddle paid no little attention to me he took my hand and led me down stairs & shok my hand cordialy,

A sarvant tried to piosen mistress & 2 3 children, what a dreadful concience she must have;

Isabella is by far too indulgent to me & even the Miss Crafords say that they wonder at her patience with me & it is indeed true for my temper is a bad one

My religion is greatly falling off because I don't pray with so much attention when I am saying my prayers & my character is lost a-mong the Breahead people I hope I will be religious agoin but as for reganing my charecter I despare for it,

*

Isa bids me give you a note of the sarman preached by Mr Bonner it was that we sould ofer ourselves to God morning & evening & then we will be happy with God if we are good

＊

At Breahead there is a number of pictures & some have monstrous large wigs;

Every body just now hates me & I deserve it for I don't behave well;

＊

I will never again trust in my own powr. For I see that I cannot be good without Gods assistence, I will trust in my selfe & it

Isas health will be quite ruined by me it will indced;

I can never repay Isabella for what she has done but by good behave-our.

If I am good I will be [happy] but if I am bad I will be unhappy

Isa has giving me advice which is that when I feal Satan beginning to tempt me that I flea from him & he would flea from me.

John is gone to Queensferry to meat ser[vent] Willman; It is far better to behave well then ill;

Let me give you a note of the sarmon it is that if we are determ[ined] to be good & try to be so that will always succeed for God when he seas that when we are trying will assist us

Many people say that it is diffic[ult] to be good but it is they will not try to do it;

The best way to be good is to pray to God to give us assistence & if he gives us assistenc I can say that I will be good & we sould never mind punishmend if it is to do us good & it is better to bare punishment if it is to save us from brimston & fire; –We are reading a book abou a man wont into a house & he saw a sack & he went & look into it & he saw a dead body in it

*

Marjory must write no more journal till she writes better[13]

Communications Expectations Forwardness

*

I know that if I try truly to be good God will healp me to be so & with his hepe alone can we behave well indeed it is true & every body will see so;

Nancy is too indulgent & Isa I could not find one like her though I was to search the [world] indeed people must say that, or they will be false people but I do not think they will be so

*

This is Thursday & it was frosty but the sun shins in all its beauty it is very romantick inded; –

Isabella & Miss Isabella Craford walks to Baron bugal[14] & jump with filisity over wals & fences; –

Life is indeed p[r]asious to thos who are good because they are hapy & good indeed.

Remorse is the worst thing to bear & I am afraid that I will fall a marter to it when I am going to Kerkaldy & to my poor mother,[15] again I will tell you why so it is that I have thrown away many advantages that athers have not therefore I I think I will fall a victom to remorse; –

There is four You treas & Is sa caled 1 of them Lot & his wife

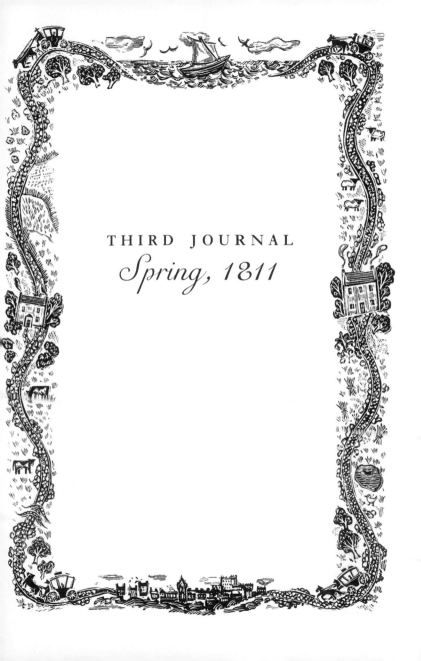

THIRD JOURNAL
Spring, 1811

I would be happy you to see
For I am sure that I love thee
You are the darling of my heart
With you I cannot bear to part
The watter falls we go to see
I am as happy as can be
In pastures sweet we go & stray
I could walk there quite well a[ll]
At night my head on turf could
There quite well could I sleep a[nd]
The moon would give its trance
I have no more of poetry
O Isa do remember me
And try to love your Marjory

Kirkaldy 26th July 1811.

. . . not be happy at the death of our fellow creatures, for they love life like us

love your neighbour & he will [love] you Bountifullness and Mercifulness are always rewarded, Isabella has admible patience in teaching me musick and resignation in perfection

In my travels I met with a handsome lad named Charles Balfour Esg, and from him I got ofers of marage. Offers of marage did I say? Nay plainly [ ] d me. —Goodness does not belong [ ] but badness dishonour befals wickedness but not virtue, no disgrace befals virtue, perciverence overcomes almost all difficulties no I am rong in saying almost I should say always, my Cosin says pacience is a cristain virtue, which is true; —fortitude is of use in time of distress, & indeed it is always of use; many people have su [ ] in mesery & have not had fortitude to suppress there . . .[1]

*

CARELESS MARJORY[2]

*

The Divil is curced & all his works. —Tis a fine book Newton on the profecies;[3] . . . anther book of poem comes near the bible; —The Divel always grins at the sight of the bibles; bibles did I say? Nay at the word virtue, I should like to learn Astronomy & Geography; —

Miss Potune is very fat she pretends to be very learned she says she saw a stone that dropt from the skies, but she is a good christian

An annibabtist is a thing I am not a member of: –I am a Pisplikan just now & a Prisbeteren at Kercaldy my native town which thugh dirty is clein in the country;

Sentiment is what I am not acquanted wth [th]ough I wish it & should [li]ke to pratise it I wish I [h]ad a great great deal [o]f gratitude in my heart [&] in all my body; –[4]

The English have great power over the franch; Ah me peradventure, at this moment some nobel Colnel at this moment sinks to the ground without breath; –& in convulsive pangs dies; it is a melancholy consideration

*

Love I think is in the fasion for ever body is marring there is a new novel published named selfcontroul[5] a very goo[d] maxam forsooth Yesterday a marrade [man] named Mr John Balfour Esg offered to kiss me, & offered to marry me though the man was espused, & his wife was prsent, & said he must ask her permision but he did not I think he was ashamed or confounded before 3 gentelman Mr Jobson & two Mr Kings Isabella teaches me to read my bible & tells me to be good and say my prayers, and every thing that is nesary for a good carecter and a good conscience. –

EPHIBOL ON MY DEAR
LOVE ISABELLA[6]

Here lies sweet Isabell in bed
With a nightcap on her head
Her skin is soft her face is fair
And she has very pretty hair
She and I in bed lies nice
And undisturbed by rats and mice
She is disgusted with Mr Wurgan
Though he plays upon the organ
A not of ribans on her head
Her cheak is tinged with concious red
Her head it rests upon a pilly
And she is not so very silly
Her nails are neat her teath are white
Her eyes are white very bright
In a conspicuos town she lives
And to the poor her money gives
Here ends sweet Isabellas story
And may it be much to her glory

All this is a true and a full discription.

*

In the love novels all the heroins are very desperate
Isabella will not alow me to speak about lovers & heroins

& tiss too refined for my taste a lodestone is a curous thing indeed it is true Heroick love doth win disgra[ce] is my maxim & I will follow it for ever &

Miss Egwards tails[7] are very good, particulay some that are very much adopted for youth as Lazy Lawrance & Tarelton False Key &c &c.– Persons of the parlement house are as I think caled Advocakes Mr Cay & Mr Crakey has that honour, This has been a very mild winter,

Mr Banestors Budjet[8] is tonight & I hope it will be a good one. –A great many authors have expressed themselfes too sentimentaly I am studying what I like, musick, Ri[c]hes Wealth & Honour are to be desired

I have seen the Wild Beasts & they are exelent particularly the Lion & hunting Tiger the Elaphant Boltcd & unbolted a door & such like wonders but of all the birds I admired the Pelecan of the Wilderness

My Aunts birds grow every day more healthy

The Mercandile Afares are in a perilious situation, sickness & a delicate frame I have not & I do not know what it is but Ah me perhaps I shall have it,

Grandure reagns in London & in Edinburgh there are a great many balls & routs but none here.

–The childish distempers are very frequent just now

Tomson is a beautifull author & Pope but nothing is like Shakepear of which I have a little knlege of

An unfortunate death James the 5 had for he died of greif.–

Macbeth is a pretty composition but an awful one Macbeth is so bad and wicked, but Lady Macbeth is so hardened in guilt she does not mind her sins & faults

The Newgate Calender[9] is very instructive, Amusing, & shews us the nesesity of doing good & not evil

Sorrow is a thing that sadines the heart & makes one grave sad & melancholy which distreses relations & friends,

The weather is very mild & serene & not like winter

*

A sailor called here to say farewell, it must be dreadfull to leave his native country where he might get a wife or perhaps me, for I love very very much & wth all my heart, but O I forgot Isabella forbid me to speak about love. –
A great many bals & routs are geven this winter & the last winter too, –Many people think beuty is better then virtue [ ] one of our beauties just now

Isabella is always reading & writing in her room, & does not come down for long & I wish every body would follow her example & be as good as pious & virtious as she is & they would get husban[ds] soon enough, love is a very papithatick thing as well as troubelsom & tiresome but O Isabella forbid me to speak about it.

General Grame[10] has defeted the Franch the Fran[ch] prisoners have made a tumbling [ ] and my cosin says it is very neat I heard that they ma[de night]caps of there blankets and bows to make them smart and shewy

My cosins are sober and well behave[d] and very gentele and meak. –I study writing & counting & deferent accomplishments

*

James Macary is to be trasported for murder in the flower of his youth[11] O passion is a terible thing for it leads people from sin to sin it gets so far as to come to greater crimes then we thought we could comit and it must be dreadfull to leave his native country and his friends and to be so disgraced and affronted.

The Spectator is a very good book as well as an instructive one Mr James and Mr John Davidson are gone to that capital town called London. –Two of the Balfours dined here yesterday and Chareles played on the flute with Isabella and they are both very handsone but John has the pleasest expression of them all but he is not instrumental which is a great loss indeed because it would afford him amusement and diversion.–

Thre are a great quantity of books selling off just now. –I am come to poo[r] Mary Queen of Scots history which Isabella explains to me and by that I understand it all or else I would not

Expostulations of all kind are very frivolous Isabella thinks this nonsense so I will say no more about Expostulations.–

The Birds do chirp the Lambs do leap and Nature is clothed with the garments of green yellow, and white, purple, and red, Many people who have money squander it all away but to do my cousins credit they do not do so or behave so improperly indeed they are not spendthrifts or persons of that sort. Good are rewarded in this wrld & the next as well as the comfort of there own consciences, love rightousness & hate evel and vice. —There is a book thats is caled the Newgate calender that contains all the Murders, —all the Murders I say, nay all Thefts & Forgeries that ever commited. & fills one with horror & consternation

Bredhede is a sweet place & in a charming situation beside wood & rivulets. —The weather is very cold & frosty & plenty of ice on the grou[nd] and on the watter Love your enemy as your friend and not as your foe this is a very windy and stormy day and looks as if it was going to snow or rain but it is only my opinion which is not always corect.—

I am reading some noveletto and one called the Pidgeon[12] is an excelent one and a charming one —I think the price of a pineapple is very dear for I here it is a whole bright goulden geinie that might have sustained a poor family a whole week and more perhaps, —Let them who temted to do wrong consider what they are about and turrn away filled with horror dread and affright There is an old Proverb which say a tile in time saves nine wich is very true indeed.—

Tawny Rachel and the Cottage cook[13] are very good excelent books and so are all the chcap Repository books indeed

Isabella is gone a tour to Melrose Abbey and I think she will be much pleased with it & I hear it is a very fine old building indeed. —In the Novellettes by Augustus Von Kot zebue I have paid particular attention to one called the Pidgeon because it is a nice and a good story

The Mr Balfours are gone far far away & I will not so much as see or hear of them anny more but I will never forget them never never

I am overpowered with the warmness of the day & the warmness of the fir[e] & it is altogether insufferable though there is a good deal of wind

Exodus & Genesis are two very good books as all the

bible is & shall be I am sure of it indeed I like the old testament better then the new but the new is far more instructive then the old.

✳

—The hedges are spruting like chicks from the eggs when they are newly hatched or as the vulgar says clacked. —I pretended to write to a lord Yesterday named Lord Roseberry[14] about killing crows & rooks that inhabit his castle or estate but we should excuse my Lord for his foolishness for as people think I think Too for people think he is a little derangeed

✳

MY ADDRESS TO ISABELLA
ON HER RETURN,

Dear Isabella you are a true lover of nature
thou layest down thy head like the meak mountain lamb
Who draws its last sob by the side of its dam,

Taken f[r]om hill Villean[15] a poem by Walter Scott & a most beautiful one it is indeed

This address I composed myself & nobody assisted me I am sure

✳

I get acquanted with boys & girls almost every day.
–wickedness and vice makes one miserable & unhappy as
well as a concousness of guilt on our mind. –Doctor
Swifts works are very funny & amusing & I get some by
hart. –Vanity is a great folly & sometimes leads to a great
sin disimulation I think is worse. This wa[s] a bad day but
now is a [good] one. Selfe-denial is a good thing and a
virtue. –St Paul was remarkable for his releigion and
piety he was in a grea[t] many pereils & dangers

*

Many people that are pretty are very vain and conceated
men praise and amire her, & some finds thcir heart ake
because of her asks her to marry him and dies if she refuses
him but is overpowered with joy if she consets to marry him
    Wallflor grows very well I think so at least.
–Moreheads Sermons are I hear much praised but I never
read Sermons of any kind but I read Novelettes and my
bible for I never forget it and it would be a sin to forget it
or my prayers either of them

*

[ ]
[the foun]dation of the barracks[16] and we will perhaps be
saccrifised to death and the grave but soulders are in
serch for them & peradvenu[re] they will be found I
sencerly wish so

The Earl of Bucan says we should take care of our charector & our health poor

*

[ ]
—tue, thou are what people like O virtue! —Meat is very [dear] nowadays. —People should not be proud or saucy or vain for vanity is a sin

All the King James died mesirable deaths one of grfe, another murdered, but Lord Darnlys was the most cruel

Mary Queen of Scots was a prisoner in Lochleven Castle. —The Casawary is an curious bird & so is the Gigantick Crane & the Pelican of the Wilderness whose mouth holds a bucket of fish & water. —Fighting is what

ladies is not gualyfied for they would not make a good
figure in battle or in a dual Alas we females are of little
use to our country & to our friends, I remember to have
read about a lady who dressed herselfe in mans cloths to
fight for her father, woman are not half so brave as her,
but it is only a story out of Mothers Gooses Fary tales so
I do not give it cridit, that is to say I do not belive the
truth of it but it matters little or nothing.

*

Last night it was very cold but this morning is very warm
it extraordinary change. —The history of all the
Malcontents that exer was hanged is very amusing I have
read some of of these larned men but they got there
reward in due form

Isabella this morning taught me some Franch words
one of which is bon suar the interpretation is good
morning.

—I like sermons better then lectures. —Joy depends
on thou O virtue!. —Tom Jones & Greys Elegey in a
contry Church yard are both excelent & much spoke of
by both sex particularly by the men.

Personal charms are as nothing if the hart is not
good & virtuous; —A person may be pretty & not good &
dutiful to her parents

Mary Queen of Scots confedrats or friens was
defeated by Murys & his associats & thought she was safe

in the castle when she effected her escape, by a young boy named Gorge Duglas;–

People who steal & murder bring eternal damnation in the next world upon them, as well as unhappiness in this world. –Adam & Eve dissibayed God. The scarlet fefer is like a plague just now.

God is the creator of us all and we should serve honour and obey him. –Isabella has often told me that, if people do not chek their passion when they are young it will grow worse and worse when they are old so that nobody will love them or obey then. –Isabella is greived when I behave ill but when I behave well she kisses and careses me and she kissed me today because I behaved well.–

God is kind and indulgent to us which we do not deserve for we are sinful creaturs & do not deserve to be so kindly treated but god does not do so. –Though we pray in publick that should not hinder us fron private prayer.

–If any mans wife marry another man when her husband is yet alive [ ]¹⁷ everbody will hate her & she shall be the object of there deristion & there disgust

The wcked are envious of the good & just & in there own plot his distruction but the lord does not leave him unpunished for if he is not punished in this world he will be punished in the next & a most terrible punishment it will be. –Macary is not yet transpor[ted] it must be a dreadful thing transportation. –God Almighty knows every thing that we do or say & he can kill you in a moment. –Bishop Sanaford[18] excels Mr James in preaching. –Lying is the high road to theft & murder King John is a beautiful play & so is King Richard the 3 I never saw a play acted in my life.

–Any body that does not do well are very very misarable & unhappy & not contented

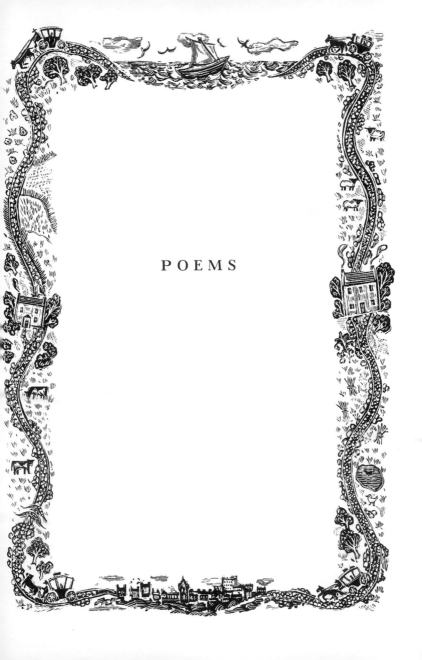

POEMS

happy. for I am

tomorrow to a deligh[t]

place, Breahead bry

belonging to Mrs C

ford, where their is a
                re   are

cocks hens bubblyjocks 2
                    &
2 cats snime. whe

delightful . I thi

it is shoking to

that the dog & ca

should bear them

they are drowned
d.

THE LIFE OF
§ MARY QUEEN OF SCOTS §
BY M. F.

Poor Mary Queen of Scots was born
With all the grace which adorn
Her birthday is so very late
That I do now forget the date
Her education was in france
There she did learn to sing & dance
There she was married to the dauphin
But soon he was laid in a coffin
Then she at once from Francretired
Where she had been so much admired
Farewell dear france she cried at last
While a desparing look she cast
The nobels came to meet there Quee[n]
Whom they before had never seen
They never saw a face so fair
For there is no such beauties there
That with her they could compair
She was a Roman Catholic strong
Nor did she think that it was wro[ng]
But they her faith could not well bear
And to upbraid her they would dare
Ther was a man that was quite good
To preach against her faith he would

His name was John Knox a reformer
Of Mary he was a great scorner
Her nation was so very feirce
That they your very hart peirce
In love she fell & deap it was
Lord Darnly was the very cause
A nobels son a handsome lad
by some queer way or other had
Got quite the better of her hart
With him she always talked apart
Silly he was but very fair
A greater buck was not found there
He was quite tall & slender too
And he could dance as well as you
Soon was the nupsials done & ore
Of it there was said nothing more
They lived togeather for a while
And happiness did there time beguile
Mary was charmed with a player
Of whom she took great care
He fed upon the finest fair
He was her greatest favourite
Him she caresed with all her might
She gave him food she gave him wine
When he was gone she would repine
The King heard this with anger sore
This is not all there is much more

For he did murder the poor player
Of whom she took so great a care
In agony she heaved a sigh
For on the King she did relie
Bad hatered at length foud a way
It was a little more then play
An awful day at last arived
Which was the last that he survived
For she went to a masqurade
But for that thing he dearly paid
For her absence what was done
The thing would not I'm sure give fun
The house in which the King did lie
I cannot think without a sigh
Was blowen up at too next day
The King was killed I'm sorry to say
Some degree of suspicion fell
On the mighty Earl of Bothwell
And of the Queen they did [think] too
That of that thing she quite well knew
For they do think that mary was
Of Darnlys death the very cause
But he was guiltless of the crime
But it was only for that time
Mary went to meet her son
That thing did not give her much fun
For Bothwell under some pretence

And with a great deal of expence
Marched to a town there found the Queen
He was quite glad when she was seen
He then disperced her slender train
That did not give her any pain
His castle of Dunbar she went
It was just there that she was sent
Poor Mary did not shew much terror
I must say this is an error
This opportunity they catched
For there they did wish to be mached
To Edinburgh the Queen was brought
He was quite glad that she was caught
The castle was then in his power
His temper was quite bad & sowr
There she was lodged in the castle
Which was as bad near as the bastile
He was then married to the Queen
Of whom he did not care a pin
The nobles formed a conspiracy
On poor Bothwell & poor Mary
Kirkaldy of grange & some more
His name I did not tell before
The nobles soldiars were quite brave
And they there masters lives would sav[e]
Poor Bothwells friends were not the same
And spread a small degree of faim

For their poor master they forsook
But in their base flight he pertook
For he said to the Queen, adieu
Those that behave so are but few
The King said to the Queen farewell
For his poor soldiers nearly fell
After Bothwell went away
In a humour not like play
She gave herselfe up with much [ease]
And she did try them all to plea[se]
The soldiers behaved very bad
It would indeed have put me ma[d]
For when she turned her eyes so bri[ght]
She always saw a dreadful sight
Darnlys Picture with her poor son
That did not give her any fun
Judge and revenge my cause cried he
This mary could not bear to see
Covered with dust droping a tear
A spectical she did appear
To break her marrage she would not
Though it would happy make her lot
This her bad nobles would not bear
Though she was then so very fair
To Lochleven was she then carried
She would not say she was not married
At last from prison she got away

She got from prison I do say
All her great arts she had employed
And the success she had enjoyed
Her keepers brother gained she had
He was a very fine young lad
At last she hinted that she would
Make him her husband if she could
On Sunday night the second of may
She did escape that very day
At supper when his brother sat
I have not got a rhyme for that
And all the family had retired
His cleverness I much admired
One of this friends stole of the keys
To let her out when she did please
Let out poor Mary & her maid
Indeed she got from him much aid
But for that thing his brother pad
She got to the boat which was prepair[ed]
Nobody but george for her cared
There she [did] meet her friends on shore
Who had been there some time before
At Setons house she sat some time
There she got good bread & good wine
She then got up & rode away
Full of gre[at] mirth & full of play
To Hamilton she came at last

For she did galop very fast
Then she her followers all prepaired
And fealy to their Queen they sweared
They marched aginst the regent who
Could perhaps fight as well as you
Mary meanwhile was on a hill
Where she did stand up quite stock still
The regent Murry ganed them all
And every one of hers did fall
She then did mount again to ride
For in her friends she couldn't confide
She flew to England for protection
For Elisbeth was her connection
Elisbeth was quite cross & sour
She wished poor Mary in her power
Elisbeth said she would her keep
And in her kingdom she might sleep
But to a prison she was sent
Elisbeths hart did not relent
Full ninteen years & mayhap more
Her legs became quite stif & sore
At last she heard she was to die
And that her soul would mount the [sky]
She was qite overjoyed at this
She thought it was her greates bliss
The hour of death at last drew nigh
When she did mount the scaffold high

Upon the block she laid her head
She was as calm as if in bed
One of the men her head did hold
And then her head was of I'm told
There ends all Queen Elisbeths foes
And those who at her bend their bows
Elisbeth was a cross old maid
Now when her youth began to fade
Her temper was worce then before
And people did not her adore
But Mary was much loved by all
Both by the great and by the small
But hark her soul to heaven did rise
And I do think she gained a prise
For I do think she would not go
Into the awfull place below
There is a thing that I must tell
Elisbeth went to fire & hell
Him who will teach her to be cevel
It must be [her great] friend the divil

§ SONNET §
To a Pug[1]

O lovely O most charming pug
Thy gracefull air & heavenly mu[g]
The beauties of his mind do shine
And every bit is shaped so fine
Your very tail is most devine
Your teeth is whiter then the snow
Yor are a great buck & a bow
Your eyes are of so fine a shape
More like a christains then an ape
His cheeks is like the roses blume
Your hair is like the ravens plume
His noses cast is of the roman
He is a very pretty weomen
I could not get a rhyme for roman
And was oblidged to call it weoman

At perth poor James the first did die
That wasn't a joy & luxery
And the poor King was murdered ther[e]
The noble to do this did dare
For he to check their power had tried
This effort made, did hurt their pride
The second James was not so good
To break his promise I knw he would
He once did say into an earl
He would not bring him into perl
He bid him come to Stirling castle
In this James behaved like a rascle
Upon the Kings word he relied
And to the castle he then hied
He to give up the confedracy
I would have don't if I was he
The earl refused to do that thing
At this furious was the King
He put his sword into his guts
And gave him many direfull cuts
His vassals all to arms ran
Their leader was a couardly man
From the feild he ran with terror
I must say this was an error
He was killed by a cannon splinter

In the middle of winter
Perhaps it was not at that time
But I could get no other rhy[me]
James the third was very mean
And with mean persons he was seen
He loved others more then his nobels
That was the cause of all his troubles
Very much he them insulted
And he seldom them consulted
For a long time this he had done
At last they got his youthfull son
And in battle he did ingage
Though he was fifteen years of a[ge]
They marched against the very K[ing]
For having been both bad & mean
James the thirds life ends this way
Of his faults take care I say
James the fourth was a charming prince
We have not got a better since
In flodden field alas fell he
The lords were vexed this to see
Thus fell a good King & a brave
He fell untimely to his grave
James the fifth loved favourites too
Which was a thing he should not do
At Pinkey were his armies killed
And with triump they were not filled

He died of grief & of dispair
His nobles for this did not care
Thus fell five Kings most crually
When I hear of them I'm ready to sigh
A king I should not like to be
I'd be frightened for a conspiracy

LETTERS
From Marjory

{ 1 }

*To her sister Isabella,
written from Edinburgh;
undated:*

My dear Isa

I now sit down on my botom[1] to answer all your kind and beloved letters which you was so good as to write to me. This is the first time I ever wrote a letter in my Life. —There are a great many Girls in the Square[2] and they cry just like a pig when we are under the painfull necessity of putting it to Death. —Miss Potune a Lady of my acquaintance praises me dreadfully. —I repeated something out of Deen Sweft and she said I was fit for the Stage and you may think I was primmed up with majestick Pride but upon my word I felt myselfe turn a little birsay[3] birsay is a word which is a word that William composed which is as you may suppose a little enraged. —This horrid fat Simpliton says that my Aunt is beautifull which is intirely impossible for that is not her nature.—

{2}

To her mother, written from Edinburgh;
original now lost;
undated:

My dear Mud,

I hope you are well: give my love to Isa and Baby, and I will send them something. I have been often at Ravelstone and once at Aunt Fleming and Mrs Miller. I've been acquainted with many very genteel girls, and Janetta is a very fine one. Help[4] is been confined another time. My sleeves is tucked up, and it was very disagreeable, my collar, and I abhorred it amoniable. I saw the most prettyist two tame pidgeons you ever saw and two very wee small kittens like our cat. I am very much acquainted with a young gentleman called Mordecai that I am quite in love with, another called Captain Bell, and

Jamie Keith, and Willie's my great tormentor. A good-natured girl gave me a song book, and I am very happy. I'll go down and be thinking when I'm eating my dinner more to tell you, Mud.

Aunt has got two of the most beautifullest Turtle Doves you ever saw. They coo for everlasting and fight. The hawk is in great spirits, it is a nice beast, the gentlest animal that was ever Seen. Six canaries, two green linnets, and a Thrush. Isa has been away for a long time

and I've been wearying for her Sadly. I like Isa and Nan very much. I play in the back green, and bring in worms for the thrush. I've done a pair of garters for Isabella but one of them is to Short. I will work it larger and work some for Nancy too. I get very long tasks, and when I behave I get them short. Orme Keir is the greatest recovery ever was, and he's thinking about business. My aunt lets the Birds to get the air in her room. The young gentleman I was speaking of Mordecai, he's very funny. James Keith hardly ever Spoke to me. he said Girl! Make less noise, and, when there was a storm sometimes said take out away all your iron, and once before he said, Madgie, go and dance, which I was very proud of. Mind my Dear Mud to return this letter when you return Isabella's. I've forgot to say, but I've four lovers, the other one is Harry Watson, a very delightful boy. Help is very like a tiger when he bites his fleas, a fine, gentle, wise creetyur. Willie was at the Moors, but he soon came back again, for the Moors was like a fish pond like Miss Whyts. I've Slept with Isabella but she cannot Sleep with me. I'm so very restless. I danced over her legs in the morning and she cried O dear you mad Girl, Madgie, for she was sleepy. The whole house plagues me about 'Come haste to the wedding', for there is no sense in it; they think, because it is an Merican, Eliza Purves taught me, they plague me about it exceeding much. I'm affronted to say it, it is so awkward.

Remember your dear Madgie.
Amen.
Finis.
M.F. six years old[5]

{3}

To her sister Isabella: incomplete:

Edinburgh 1 April 1811

My dear Isabella

I hear that your health has been declining of late I was greatly dissapointed that you did not come over I should have been so happy to see you I send you an orange I got at General Diroms[6] where I was drinking tea I am studying much at present and I hope improving my mind, –a new cousin of mine offered me marriage and his name is Charels Balfour and he is handsome to excess

{4}

To Isabella Keith; from Kirkcaldy;
dated 26 July, 1811:

I am now in my native land
And see my dear friends all at hand
There is a thing that I do want
With you the beauteous walks to haun[t]
We would be happy if you would
Try to come over if you could
Then I would quite happy be
Now & for all eternity
Isa is so very kind
A better girl I could not find

My mother is so very sweet
And checks my appetite to eat
My father shews us what to do
But I am sure that I want you
I would be happy you to see
For I am sure that I love thee
You are the darling of my heart
With you I cannot bear to part
The watter falls we go to see
I am as happy as can be
In pastures sweet we go & stray
I could walk there quite well all day
At night my head on turf could lay
There quite well could I sleep all night
The moon would give its tranciant light
I have no more of poetry
O Isa do remember me
And try to love your Marjory

Kirkaldy 26 July 1811.

{5}

To Isabella Keith;
dated 1 September, 1811:

My Dear little Mama

I was truly happy to hear that you are all well. My mother bid me tell you that you are delaying your visit to long for you will not get out which will be a hard restrait to you. We are surrounded with measles at present on every side for the Herons got it an Isabella Heron was near deaths door and one night her father lifted her out of bed And she fell down as they thou[ght] lifeless Mr Heron said that lassie is dead now she said I'm no dead yet she then threw up a big worm nine inches and a half long. My Mother regrets she cannot write to you at present as her eyes are very sore. I have begun dancing but am not very fond of it for the boys strikes and mocks me. I have been another night at the dancing & like it better. I will write to you as often as I can but I am afraid I shall not be able to write you every [week]

I long for you with the longings of a child to embrace you to fold you in my arms I respect you with respect due to a mother. You don't know how I love you so I shall remain your loveng child M Fleming

Kirkaldy Septr. 1st. 1811

{6}

To Isabella Keith;
dated 12 October, 1811:

My Dear Mother

You will think that I entirely forget you but I assure you that you are greatly mistaken. I think of you allways and often sigh to think of the distance between us two loving creatures of nature

We have regular hours for all ours occupations first at 7 oclock we go to the dancing and come home at 8 we then read our bible and get our repeating then we play till 10 then we get our musick till 11 when we get our writing an accounts we sew from 12 till 1 & play till dinner after which I get my gramer and then work till five at 7 we come & knit till 8 when we don't go to the dancing this is an exact description of our employments.

You have disappointed us all very much especially me in not coming over every coach I heard I ran to the window but I was always disapointed I must take a hasty farewell to her whom I love reverence & doat on and who I hope thinks the same of Marjory Fleming.

P S An old pack of cards would be very exeptible

Kirkaldy 12 Octr 1811.

{7}

To Isabella Keith at Braehead; delivered by
Marjory's brother William. Undated, but answered
by Isabella in November 1811:

My Dear Isa

I wish I was William that I might see you. I have a musick book for the violoncello and harpsichord and a sermon book which I would have sent to you if my mother said to ask you first if you would take it

Tell the Miss Crawfurds that I always remember them Tell the eldest that I keep the box as a Memento Mori adieu dear Isa

P S Write the first & last verse of hill valen[7] again ad[ieu]

{8}

To Isabella Keith, back in Edinburgh;
dated November 1811; incomplete:

. . . loving. She is quite sirprised that she has not hard from any of you on which I will compose the following poem

> *O Isa why do you not write*
> *I'm out of mind when out of [sight]*
> *I am afraid your dead & gone*

And thus I do begin my moa[n]
O miresable unhappy chi[ld]
To lose a mistress meak & mild
With all the graces which adorn
I wish that I was never born
I cannot bear the thought O no
Indeed I wish it was not so
Thine eyes with luster will not [spark]
And in the grave where it is [dark]
Thow shalt be layed a lady fa[ir]
It fills my hart with great dis[pair]
Indeed I now must say adie[u]
Both to Isabel and you

{9}
To Isabella Keith, 15 December 1811;
written four days before her death:

§ ADDRESS TO DEAR ISABELLA §
ON THE AUTHORS RECOVERY

O Isa pain did visit me
I was at the last extremity
How often did I think of you
I wished your graceful form to view
To clasp you in my weak embrace
Indeed I thought Id run my race.

Good care Im sure was of me taken
But indeed I was much shaken
At last I daily strength did gain
And O at last away went pain
At length the docter thought I might
Stay in the Parlour till the night
I now continue so to do
Farewell to Nancy and to you.

Wrote by M F.

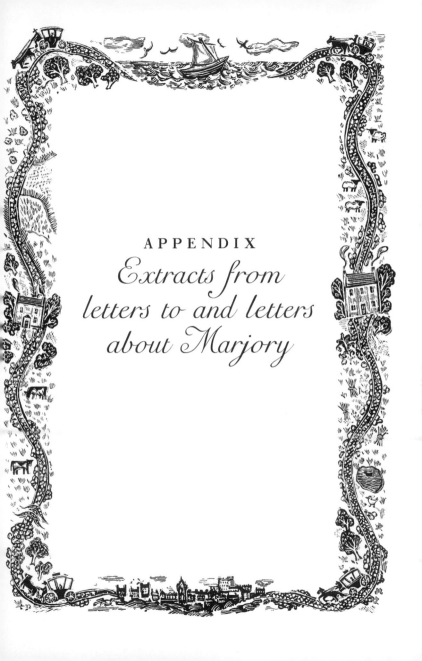

APPENDIX

Extracts from letters to and letters about Marjory

From Isabella Keith to Marjory's sister
Isabella; dated 1 April 1811:

My Dear Isabella

I hope you will excuse the shortness of Maidie's letter and trusting to a longer one from her soon accept of a few lines from me instead, – she is going on very busily with her lessons in all of which she is I hope improving, except her musick she dislikes it so much that she loses all patience, but I hope when she gets the length of playing a Tune she will like it better and pay more attention. – She is very fond of History and is reading the history of Scotland at present in which she is much interested. She continues her journal every day entirely by herself it is a very amusing production indeed, and when finished I shall send it over for your Mothers perusal, and I hope she will find it more correct and better written than the last. I have almost entirely given up her dancing, as it took up a great deal too much time, and a few lessons a year or two after this will do her infinitely more good, she is grown excessively fat and strong, but I cannot say she is in great beauty just now, as she has lost her two front teeth, and her continual propensity to laugh exhibits the defect rather unbecomingly. I have now I think said enough of our dear Muffy, and will talk of other matters . . .

From Isabella Keith to Marjory.
The 'Isa' referred to is Marjory's sister.
Dated November 1811:

My dear Marjory,

I take the opportunity of your brother Williams going over to write you a few lines, which I hope you will not delay answering. I cannot see that a letter once a week can be a great hardship to you as it might serve instead of your writing Lesson, and you will always find plenty to say if you tell me about your Mother your Sisters and Yourself: –

I am still enjoying this delightful weather at sweet Braehead. Margaret has been rather delicate a few weeks past, and is not able to take long walks, but Isabella and I go to Barnbougle and the Seaside every day, I very often take my little glass and look over to Kirkaldie, I see Raith Tower perfectly plainly, and I would see Kirkaldie too were it not situated in the bay. This would be very pleasant, for with a telescope I could distinguish the figures on the opposite side of the water and then I might perhaps see you and Isa at play in the fields, only I am afraid I might sometimes be vexed by observing your behaviour to gentle Isa which I am sorry to hear is not exactly what it ought to be do you remember what conversations you and I used to have on this subject?

—and how often you assured me you were sorry for having been cross to Isabella when you were young, and that you were resolved you should always for the future be kind and obedient to her. I hope in your next Letter you will be able to tell me you are trying to be mild and tractable and good humoured.

I long much my dear daughter to see you and talk over all our old stories together, and to hear you read and repeat. I am tiring for my old friend Cesario, and for poor Lear, and wicked Richard: –how is the dear Multiplication Table going on, –are you still as much attached to 9 times 9 as you used to be?–

I have not Helvellyn here but I think I can remember it by heart pretty correctly: –

[*Here Isabella quotes the whole of Scott's poem*]

May and Isy Crawfurd send their love and a Kiss to you. I wish I had you by me, and I would give you twenty myself farewell my dear Muff don't forget your Isabella . . . I opened my letter again to say how much I am obliged to you for the offer of the Sermons and the Music book. If it is not robbing your Mother or yourself I would receive them with great gratitude . . .

3

From Mrs Fleming to Isabella Keith;
dated 9 January 1812:

You will not be surprised my beloved Isabella that after the various fears anxieties and agitations which have harassed my mind for Eight years past my body should sink under a stroke so sudden, so severe . . . You more than anyone else can imagine and sympathise in the blank I feel . . . Her constant good humour gave a chearfulness to our domestic circle which made us feel no want of society. Her poor Father unceasingly deplores his loss, I fear he idolised her too much and was too vain of her talents, besides death was a scene altogether new to him – and oh how striking was her death . . .

To tell you what poor Maidie said of you would fill volumes, for you was the constant theme of her discourse, the subject of her thoughts, and ruler of her actions – for what would reflect credit or reproach on your tuition were the motives by which she was chiefly actuated or restrained, and I loved her the more for the affection she bore you, which was truly filial. The last time she mentioned you was a few hours before all sense save that of suffering was suspended when she said to Dr Johnstone 'If you will let me out at the New Year I will be quite contented.' I asked what made her so anxious to get out then: she replied 'I wish to purchase a new years gift for

Isa Keith with the Sixpence you gave me for being patient during the Measles, and would like to chuse it myself.' I do not recollect her speaking afterwards except to complain of her poor head, till just before she expired when she articulated oh Mother Mother. I send wt this what she esteemed most her Bibles for you and pocket book for Nancy . . . Write to me soon, it is my greatest comfort . . .

{4}

From Isabella Keith to Mrs Fleming;
written some time in January after the above:

. . . though I hope I am perfectly resigned to the will of the Almighty . . . my mind still dwells too much on her sufferings, & her Death . . . I have all her writing copies, spelling book, and many other little trifles which I collected after she left me, any of which or even her journals, much as I value all of them, if you wish for them I shall part with but only to her Mother will I ever relinquish the smallest trifle that ever belonged to her. When Time shall have a little blunted the immediate bitterness of feeling, they will be a source of melancholy pleasure to me . . . her bibles are precious to me . . . their dear possessor is now in the enjoyment of that Elysian bliss which every page holds out . . . and through whose merits I hope again to see my beloved Maidie . . .

From Elizabeth Fleming to
Dr John Brown; about 1863:

. . . I believe she was a child of robust health, of much vigour of body, and beautifully formed arms, and until her last illness, never was an hour in bed . . . As to my aunt and Scott, they were on a very intimate footing . . . I have to ask you to forgive my anxiety in gathering up the fragments of Marjory's last days . . . Measles were the cause of her death. My mother was struck by the patient quietness manifested by Marjorie during this illness, unlike her ardent, impulsive nature: but love and poetic feeling were unquenched . . . when lying very still, her mother asked her if there was anything she wished: 'Oh, yes! If you would just leave the room door open a wee bit, and play "The Land o' the Leal", and I will lie and think, and enjoy myself' . . . Well, the happy day came, alike to parents and child, when Marjorie was allowed to come forth from the nursery to the parlour. It was Sabbath evening, and after tea. My father, who idolised this child, and never afterwards in my hearing mentioned her name, took her in his arms; and while walking her up and down the room, she said, 'Father, I will repeat something to you; what would you like?' He said, 'Just choose yourself, Maidie.' She hesitated a moment between the paraphrase, 'Few are thy days and full of woe,' and the lines of Burns already quoted, but decided on the latter, a remarkable choice for a child. The repeating these lines seemed to stir up the depths of feeling in her soul. She asked to be allowed to write a poem; there was a doubt whether it would be right to allow her, in case of hurting her eyes. She pleaded earnestly, 'Just this once.' The point was yielded, her slate was given her, and with great rapidity she wrote an address of fourteen lines, 'to her loved Cousin on the author's recovery', her last work on earth: – 'Oh! Isa, pain did visit me . . .'

She went to bed apparently well, awoke in the middle of the night with the old cry of woe to a mother's heart, 'My head, my head!' Three days of the dire malady, 'water in the head', followed, and the end came.

AFTERWORD

...ret quiet frienship books, a...
dwell here but I am not sure...
and alternate labour useful t...

I leaven Isa's bed to lie

O such a joy & luxury
The bottom of the bed I sleep
And with great care I ne'er s...
Oft I embrace her feet of lillys
But she has gotten all the pillies
Her neck I never can embra...
But I do hug her feet in plac...
But I am sure I am contea...
And of my folliesum repent...

Marjory Fleming was born in Kirkcaldy, Fife, on 15 January 1803, into an educated middle-class family. Her father James was an accountant, local councillor and magistrate; her uncle was a minister. Her mother, born Isabella Rae, came from a cultured Edinburgh family, with a strong scientific streak: her father and two brothers were surgeons. On this side of the family there was a distant connection by marriage to Walter Scott.

The Fleming household comprised James and Isabella, and the children William (born 1798), Isabella (born 1800), Marjory and Elizabeth (born in 1809 when Marjory was nearly seven). Not long after the birth of this new baby, Marjory was taken to stay with her mother's sister, Marianne Keith, who lived in the New Town of Edinburgh at 1 North Charlotte Street. This visit turned out to be a prolonged one, for apart from a possible trip in the autumn of 1810, she did not return home to live until her eighth year in July 1811. It may seem a strange thing to us that a young child should be away from her mother at such an early age, but we must remember that protracted family visits were then quite common. Perhaps the intention was to give Mrs Fleming a little breathing space after the birth of her new baby. She may have suffered from ill-health, or what we now call post-natal depression. In a letter to her niece written just after Marjory's death, she referred to 'the various fears anxieties and agitations which have harassed my mind for Eight years past.'

In any case, Marjory lived away from home for over a year, mainly in the 'conspicuos town' of Edinburgh, with her widowed aunt Marianne and her cousins Nancy, James, William and, most importantly, Isabella (or 'Isa'), who was then about twenty-two years old. They also made long visits to the country: Braehead House near Cramond was the home of Mrs Keith's friends the Craufurd family, and a place of 'rurel filisity'; likewise the home of Mrs Keith's in-laws at Ravelston. Wherever she went, Isabella was her constant companion.

Somehow, it was decided that Isabella would take charge of Marjory's education. The journals were almost certainly her idea, and they were written under her watchful eye: 'Isabella campels me to sit down & not rise till this page is done . . .' Isabella was more than a teacher to Marjory, she became an affectionate friend and even a mother figure. Marjory adored her. A picture emerges through Marjory's eyes of Isabella – a patient, wise, attractive, conscientious young woman, who not only taught 'reading writing and arithmetic', but 'religion into the bargain' and 'everything that is nesary for a good carecter and a good conscience.'

Together they studied history. Marjory's imagination was so fired by the story of 'poor' Mary Queen of Scots that she wrote a long rhyming account of her life.

Arithmetic had to be tackled, but it was not her favourite subject: 'I am now going to tell you about the horrible and wretched plaege that my multiplication gives me you cant conceive it – the most Devilish thing is 8 times 8 & 7 times 7 it is what nature itselfe cant endure.' Nor did she enjoy lessons in music: Isabella wrote to Marjory's sister, 'She dislikes it so much that she loses all patience.' Her studies in French were not wholly successful: 'Isabella this morning taught me some French words one of which is bon suar the interpretation is good morning . . .' There were lessons in handwriting, spelling, and punctuation to be endured, also with somewhat mixed results: 'Isa is teaching me to make Simecolings nots of interrgations peorids & commoes.' But literature she loved with a passion. She was a voracious reader with an eclectic taste. She read the poetry of Pope, Burns, Thomson, Gray and Scott – the latter's 'Helvellyn' was a particular favourite. She read Swift, Shakespeare, *The Arabian Nights*, Gothic romances, moral tales, stories of dastardly deeds and their punishment in *The Newgate Calendar*, the Bible, especially the Old Testament – all these stimulated her mind. Her critical comments on what she read could be very astute: 'In the love novels all the heroins are very desperate' and 'A great many authors have expressed themselfes too sentimentaly.' Her love of words is evinced by an exuberant use of language remarkable in a seven-year-old. 'Accomplishments', 'expostulations', 'consternation', 'majestick', 'stupendous', 'fabulous', even appear correctly spelled, and she made a brave stab at other words of similar magnitude: 'declifities', 'filisity', 'tempestious', 'unquenchiable', to name but a few. There are occasional happy hybrids: 'Love is a very papithatick thing'; 'Ephibol on my dear love Isabella', as well as near misses, as in her informative doctrinal aside: 'I am a Pisplikan just now & a Prisbeteran at Kercaldy.'

Religious instruction was naturally an important ingredient of her educational diet, and the journals are peppered with moral aphorisms and with Marjory's own comments on the Bible, God and the Devil. To an impressionable young mind, the image of the Devil going about 'like a roaring lyon in search of his pray' must have been the stuff of nightmares, but she consoled herself with the happy thought that at least 'satan has not geven me boils'. Isabella's religious input can frequently be discerned: 'Isabella says that when we pray we should pray fervently & not rattel over a prayer when our thoughts are wandering . . .' and 'As this is Sunday I must begin to write serious thoughts as Isabella bids me . . . on Sunday she teaches me to be virtuous.' More than a century later, Mark Twain commented on her 'little perfunctory pieties' thus:

> Under pressure of a pestering sense of duty, she heaves a shovelful of trade godliness into her

journals every little while, but it does not offend, for none of it is her own, it is all borrowed, it is a convention, a custom of her environment, it is the most innocent of hypocrisies, and this tainted butter of hers soon gets to be as delicious to the reader as are the stunning and worldly sincerities she splatters around it every time her pen takes a fresh breath.

Marjory recorded her occasional outbursts of temper with disarming honesty. These tantrums happened mostly at Braehead, and are the theme of much of the second journal. This probably explains why so many pages of her second journal have been deliberately cut or torn away. It was at Braehead that she called the unlucky John – a servant? – 'a Impudent Bitch'; there she threw her book at Isabella 'in a dreadful passion'; there she 'roared like a bull and would not go to bed'. Her subsequent remorse and sincere resolutions to be a better person were likewise faithfully noted: 'Every body just now hates me & I deserve it for I don't behave well; 'I am going to turn over a new life & am going to be . . . obedient to Isa Keith;' 'Remorse is the worst thing to bear & I am afraid that I will fall a marter to it.'

These are weighty adult matters for a seven-year-old to wrestle with, but, fortunately, her natural ebullience kept returning. She wrote about the things she loved –

the countryside, summer weather and animals. In town, at Ravelston, and particularly at Braehead, she was surrounded by a varied menagerie: there was Help the dog (a 'wise creetyur'), a 'charming' monkey and an assortment of pigs, hens, turkeys and cats, 'they are the delight of my heart'. She wrote in passionate praise of the people she loved, most notably 'sweet Isabella', but also the various 'well-made Bucks' who crossed her path. Isabella tried to discourage these childish infatuations, but try as she might Marjory couldn't help writing about them. Only rarely did she express disapproval of another: the unfortunate Miss Potune, who 'pretends to be very learned' earned her displeasure and was condemned as a 'horrid fat Simpleton', also causing Marjory to 'turn a little birsay'. (It is interesting to note how few Scots words she used in her writings, as by that time the middle classes and gentry had mostly abandoned Scotticisms.)

Marjory sometimes turned a critical eye upon her own appearance: 'I am very strong & robust & not . . . of the fair but of the deficient in look,' though there was some slight consolation in the reflection that 'people who are deficient in looks can make up for it by virtue.' We have only one contemporary description of Marjory, from Isabella herself, and it, too, indicates an appearance of vigorous health:

. . . she is grown excessively fat and strong, but I cannot say she is in great beauty just now, as she has lost her two front teeth, and her continual propensity to laugh exhibits the defect rather unbecomingly.

By the summer of 1811, Marjory was back in Kirkcaldy with her family, and the journals ended. She continued with her lessons, though without Isabella. She badly missed her cousin, as the five surviving letters from Marjory to Isabella most movingly show, but they were not to meet again. Just five months after her home-coming, she fell victim to an outbreak of measles, and died on 19 January, probably of meningitis. She was not quite nine.

Soon after this, a grief-stricken Isabella submitted Marjory's now doubly precious papers to Mrs Fleming, writing 'only to her Mother will I ever relinquish the smallest trifle that ever belonged to her'. At the request of James Fleming she made a watercolour sketch of Marjory from memory. The papers and portrait were carefully preserved by her family as treasured keepsakes, and they remained in private hands until 1930, when they were gifted to the National Library of Scotland.

Nearly fifty years after Marjory Fleming's death, a London-based Scottish journalist named Farnie was shown her journals by her surviving family, and he wrote an article about her for *The Fife Herald*, which then became a pamphlet entitled *Pet Marjorie: A Story of Child Life Fifty Years Ago*. It contained very limited extracts from the journals, interspersed with a sentimental account of her life. A later editor commented drily: 'It is enough to say of his publication that everything readable in it is Marjory's own.' Farnie's lasting legacy was in bestowing the spurious nickname 'Pet Marjorie': in reality she was familiarly called Maidie, Madgie and (by Isabella) Muffy.

However, a much more influential invention was about to appear. Farnie's booklet caught the attention of a more prominent and popular author, Dr John Brown, who subsequently brought out his own version of Marjory's life, and selected (and censored) extracts from her journals. To this end, he too gained access to the original papers and transcribed them, though not very accurately. He also corresponded with Marjory's surviving sister Elizabeth, who was only two at the time of Marjory's death. Elizabeth Fleming related to him that her aunt, Marianne Keith, and Walter Scott 'were on a very intimate footing', and that at some time Scott had presented Marjory with a couple of children's books.

These somewhat sketchy titbits excited Dr Brown into a positive frenzy of creation: his book *Pet Marjorie* opens with an entirely fanciful account of Scott carrying her off 'in the neuk of his plaid' to his study, where he and 'his warm, plump little play-fellow' would read and laugh for hours on end, and of Scott making her recite lines from Shakespeare 'till he swayed to and fro, sobbing his fill'.

Brown's book was an enormous success, appearing as it did at a time when Scott was at the height of his popularity. The winning combination of images, the 'rosy wee wifie' destined to die young, sitting on the knee of 'the Great Magician', was guaranteed to appeal to Victorian sensibilities. More than half a century later, a new edition of Lachlan Macbean's *The Story of Pet Marjorie* was subtitled *The Wonderful Playmate of Sir Walter Scott*, and advertised as 'a book that will be very welcome to all lovers of Sir Walter Scott.' (1920 edition.) Mark Twain, too, fell under the spell cast by Brown's wondrous web, although he at least showed a spirited appreciation of Marjory's own talents, one refreshingly not dependent on her putative friendship with Scott. In 1934, a later editor, Arudell Esdaile, expressed serious doubts about the truth of Brown's effusions, and made the laconic comment: 'We may allow ourselves at least a hope that [Scott] did not call Marjory "my bonny wee croodlin' doo"', but it was not until 1947 that a thorough demolition of Brown's account was undertaken. The scholar responsible, Frank Gent, concluded soberly 'no one can say they never met', but that the Keiths and the Scotts 'moved in different circles, and . . . their meetings were infrequent.' The plain fact is that Scott never mentioned Marjory in his letters, and Marjory refers to him only as the author of a poem she loved. Brown's story, cloying and fanciful though it was, nevertheless was remarkably influential while it held sway, and he must be credited for spreading her fame.

When, at last, the journals were handed over to the National Library of Scotland in 1930, it became possible to examine the original manuscripts. Four years later, and more than a century after they were written, the complete 'works' were published for the first time (in two editions, one in large-format facsimile for collectors), thus finally enabling Marjory to speak for herself. Her new editors revealed a truer picture by clarifying many hitherto confused details and removing the thick fog of Victorian sentimentality that had clouded her image. However, these scholarly works were not aimed at the general reader, and soon were out of print.

The legend of 'Pet Marjorie' may have waned, but the steady trickle of magazine and newspaper articles that have appeared over the years testify to her enduring appeal. This new edition gives today's reader a long overdue opportunity to enjoy all that was 'wrote by M.F.' – the inimitable Marjory Fleming.

§ POSTSCRIPT §

Marjory Fleming's birthplace, 130 High Street in Kirkcaldy, no longer exists, but it is still possible to see her original gravestone – simply inscribed M:F 1811 – in Abbotshall Churchyard. Adjacent, there is a statue dedicated to her as the 'Youngest Immortal', erected in 1930. A short walk away, Kirkcaldy Museum has a small collection of objects once owned by Marjory including her copy of the Bible inscribed by her mother, while her journals are held in the National Library of Scotland. Marianne Keith's house in North Charlotte Street still stands. Braehead House in Barnton is recognisable, though later additions have altered its original shape. Close by in Braepark Road there is a plaque, a memento of Marjory's happy attachment to Braehead.

NOTES

1. 'nettel Geramem': Nettle Geranium, a common name no longer in use for an indoor plant, possibly a Coleus.

2. *Tales from Fashionable Life* by Maria Edgeworth, 1809.

3. 'Osians poems': James MacPherson, the eighteenth-century poet, brought out several volumes of verse purporting to be translations from the Gaelic bard, Ossian.

4. 'the Exebition': an exhibition of paintings by the Associated Society of Artists, held in Henry Raeburn's Gallery, York Place, Edinburgh, in April 1810.

5. 'Tomsons him to the seasons': James Thomson's series of poems *Seasons*, published between 1726 and 1730. The 'unhappy lover' Celadon, to whom Marjory refers, appears in the poem 'Summer'.

6. 'A Mr Burn writs a beautifull song on a Mr Cunhaming . . .': Which poem by Robert Burns for his friend Alexander Cunningham Marjory means is a matter of conjecture; possibly 'She's Fair and Fause', or 'Ye Flowery Banks'. In any case, the theme of a true lover being ill-rewarded captured her imagination.

7. 'the Fabulous historys': a popular children's book of the time by Sarah Trimmer, *Fabulous Histories, designed for the Instruction of Children respecting their treatment of animals*, 1786.

8. 'Genius Demedicus': probably the 'Venus de Medici'.

9. Tales of the Castal': stories by the Countess de Genlis, *Tales of the Castle*.

10. 'My health is always bad and sore': just for the purpose of the rhyme, for Marjory was by all accounts a vigorously healthy child until her fatal illness.

11. 'the misteris of udolpho': Ann Radcliffe's popular Gothic tale of terror and romance *The Mysteries of Udolpho*, 1794.

12. ' . . . the Kings Birthday': George III, whose birthday in 1810 coincided with celebrations to mark his fiftieth year as King.

13. 'At Breahead I lay at the foot of the bed . . .' Marjory has written this explanatory footnote upside down in her journal.

14. 'I have been a Naughty Girl': the first of these lines is written by Isabella for Marjory to copy.

15. 'There fellow pows': pout is an old Scots word for a young bird.

16. 'the fasts by good Nelson': Robert Nelson's *Companion for the Festivals and Fasts of the Church of England*, first published in 1704, and reprinted many times.

§SECOND JOURNAL §

1. Marjory was living at Braehead House, near Cramond, with Isabella during most of the summer of 1810. Her hostess was Mrs Craufurd who had two daughters, Margaret and Isabella. There was at least one visit to Ravelston to see Isabella's grandparents.

2. 'I walked to Crakeyhall': Craigiehall, a fine mansion near Barnton, within walking distance of Braehead, now part of Army HQ, Scotland. In Marjory's time it was possibly the home of the 'well made Buck' George Craigie.

3. 'Wednesday . . . Thursday July 12th': The original journal bears entries for each date in Isabella's handwriting, which have been deliberately obliterated. The word 'Marjory' can be deciphered in several places, otherwise the content remains illegible.

4. 'Tuesday 4 . . . Wednesday': written by Isabella.

5. 'To Day I have been very ungrateful . . . .where I stood trying to open . . .' The page has been cut after the word 'open'.

6. ' . . . what nature itselfe cant endure': Two-thirds of this page has been cut out.

7. 'sina tea': Marjory is blaming her bad mood on senna tea, made from the dried leaves of the shrub senna, then commonly used as a laxative.

8. 'Haman . . . hanged on a garows': The story is in the Old Testament, Esther, Chs 7–9.

9. 'I hope that Isabella will have the goodness to teach me . . . ': In the original Marjory first wrote 'think'. The substitution of the word 'hope' above it looks like Marjory's own correction rather than Isabella's.

10. 'bublyjocks': bubblyjock is a Scots word for male turkey.

11. ' . . . it is aways spitring but then I get a blink . . . ': Marjory is disappointed when it is spitting with rain, but happy when she gets a blink of sunshine.

12. 'I am going to tell you . . . it will never happen again': this page has been partly cut away.

13. '*Marjory must write no more journal till she writes better*': in Isabella's hand. '*Communications Expectations Forwardness*' Each word is written once by Isabella, followed by a page and a half of Marjory's copies.

14. 'Baron bugal': Barnbougle Castle, a tower house on the shore of the Firth of Forth, within walking distance of Braehead. The original sixteenth-century building no longer exists.

15. ' . . . when I am going to Kerkaldy & to my poor mother': It is possible that Marjory did make a trip back home in the time which elapsed between the end of the second journal and the beginning of the

third. Her Bible, a gift from her mother, is inscribed with the date 'September 1810'.

§ THIRD JOURNAL §

1. In the original, a portion of this page is torn. Empty brackets indicate missing words.
2. 'Careless Marjory': a piece of self-criticism written in very large letters.
3. 'Tis a fine book Newton on the profecies': Possibly Sir Isaac Newton's *Observations upon the Prophecies*, 1733, but as Sidgwick suggests it is more likely to refer to *Dissertation on the Prophecies* by Thomas Newton, first published in 1754–58, and reissued in 1804.
4. '[th]ough'; '[li]ke'; '[h]ad' etc.: The bottom left-hand margin of this page is missing in the original.
5. 'there is a new novel published named selfcontroul . . .': *Self-Control* by Mary Brunton, 1811.
6. 'Ephibol on my dear love Isabella': In an unknown hand in the original there is written above this tribute to Isa 'composed & written at the age of six years'. However, this does not tally with the other indications of dating. In any case, along with 'Three Turkeys Fair' it has become one of Marjory's most famous verses, and both have been put to music by two composers, Robert McLeod and Richard Rodney Bennett.

7. 'Miss Egwards tails': Maria Edgeworth, a popular novelist of the time, wrote *Moral Tales* (1801) and *Popular Tales* (1804).

8. 'Mr Banestors Budjet': John Bannister was a comedian who toured Britain with his show 'Bannister's Budget'.

9. 'The Newgate Calender is very instructive . . .': Published under various titles from the early eighteenth century, *The Newgate Calendar* was a series of accounts of 'Murders . . . Thefts & Forgeries' and their resultant trials. Marjory found a double satisfaction here, for as well as being pleasurably frightening they taught 'the necesity of doing good & not evil'.

10. 'General Grame': Sir Thomas Graham, who led a successful military campaign against the French at Barossa in March 1811.

11. 'James Macary is to be transported for murder': James McArra of Cramond was convicted for murdering his brother and sentenced to banishment in February 1811.

12. 'the Pidgeon': A story by the German dramatist Augustus von Kotzebue.

13. 'Tawny Rachel and the Cottage cook': *Tawny Rachel, or the Fortune-Teller*, and *The Cottage Cook, or Mrs Jones's Cheap Dishes*, two novelettes from a series of morality tales entitled the Cheap

Repository by Hannah More, which appeared between 1797 and 1800.

14. 'I pretended to write to a lord . . . named Lord Roseberry': the third Earl of Roseberry, of Dalmeny Park, near Braehead.

15. 'hill Villean': Scott's 'Helvellyn', a favourite poem of Marjory's.

16. ' . . . dation of the barracks . . . ': A portion of this page is missing in the original. It is generally accepted that Marjory refers to an incident in April 1811 when about fifty French prisoners-of-war escaped from Edinburgh Castle. One was killed while manoevering himself down the castle rock; the rest were at large for a while until their eventual recapture. Robert Louis Stevenson later used the episode in his novel *St Ives*.

17. ' . . . yet alive [ ] everybody will hate her': here a line has been deleted.

18. 'Bishop Sanaford': Daniel Sandford, (1766–1830) Bishop of Edinburgh at the time.

§ POEMS §

1. To a Pug: the subject of Marjory's sonnet is the Keith's pet monkey, who was clearly a popular attraction – 'The monkey gets as many visitors as I or my cousins.'

§ LETTERS §

1. 'I now sit down on my botom . . .': An example of editorial censorship – the phrase 'on my botom' was deemed unsuitable by both Farnie and Brown, and did not appear until Macbean's book on Marjory in 1904.

2. 'the Square': Charlotte Square, just across the road from Marjory's aunt's house in North Charlotte Street.

3. 'birsay': birsie is a Scots word for hot-tempered.

4. 'Help is been confined another time': Help is the Keith's dog.

5. 'M.F. six years old': The original letter is lost. Both Brown and later Macbean made copies, but there is no way of checking the accuracy of their transcripts. It is very likely that 'six years old' was added later and incorrectly dated

6. 'at General Diroms': Alexander Dirom (1757–1830) was a Major-General in 1811 and, later, in 1813, became a Lieutenant-General.

7. 'hill valen': Scott's poem 'Helvellyn', also referred to in the third journal.

§BIBLIOGRAPHY §

H.B. Farnie: *Pet Marjorie: a Story of Child Life Fifty Years Ago*. (Edinburgh: W.P. Nimmo, 1858)

Dr John Brown: *Pet Marjorie* (Edinburgh: Edmonston and Douglas, 1863)

Lachlan Macbean: *The Story of Pet Marjorie* (London: Simpkin, Marshall, Hamilton, Kent & Co., 1904)

Mark Twain: 'Marjory Fleming, the Wonder Child' (*Harper's Bazaar*, 1909); reprinted in *The Complete Essays of Mark Twain* (ed. Charles Neider, New York: Doubleday & Co. Inc., 1963)

Frank Sidgwick: *The Complete Marjory Fleming* (London: Sidgwick & Jackson Ltd., 1934)

Arundell Esdaile: *The Journals, Letters, and Verses of Marjory Fleming in Collotype Facsimile* (London: Sidgwick & Jackson Ltd., 1934)

Frank Gent: 'Marjory Fleming and her Biographers' (in *The Scottish Historical Review*, vol. xxvi, pp 93–104, 1947)

§FURTHER READING §

Oriel Malet: *Marjory Fleming* (London: Faber & Faber, 1946)

Marion Walker: 'The Youngest Immortal' (*The Scots Magazine*, June 1953, p 170)

Douglas Guthrie: 'Marjory Fleming, "the youngest immortal"' (*The Scotsman*, Nov 9, 1963)

Carol McNeill: 'Marjory Fleming – Myths and Mists' (*The Library Review*, Winter 1971)

A.E. Graham: 'Scotland's Youngest Writer?' (*The Scots Magazine*, August 1979)

Carl MacDougall: 'Pet Marjory' (*Scottish Field*, February 1989)

Margaret MacDougall: 'A Forgotten Fife Bairn' (*The Scottish Book Collector*, vol 3, no 2, Dec 1992)